My First Ocean Animals

W. Books

Sharks have a lot of very sharp teeth!

When an octopus is scared, it can squirt out black ink;

they have eight arms and are smarter than you think!

A seahorse surprisingly can't swim very fast.

Crabs walk side to side
and sometimes they pinch!

Shrimps can be quite small; some are smaller than an inch!

Oysters have a secret that they hide.
They hold a sparkly pearl inside!

Clams and mussels can grow pearls too. They make beautiful jewelry for me and you.

Whales are very large but they're gentle as can be.

Turtles can walk on land and swim in the sea!

If you see a jellyfish, be careful not to touch;

they're cute but can sting and it hurts very much!

A starfish usually has 5 arms, but sometimes they have more.

You can find a school of stingrays roaming on the ocean floor.

A pufferfish is small but they expand when they're scared.

They're poisonous creatures, so all should beware!

The sea is full of creatures of all shapes and sizes. And all of the animals are full of surprises.

Which sea creature is your favorite?